INA MEMOIR 2024

A Life of Simplicity, Elegance, and Culinary Mastery

JAMIE C. RIDER

All rights reserved.

No part of this publication may be reproduced, distributed, or transmitted in any form or by any means, including photocopying, recording, or other electronic or mechanical methods, without the prior written permission of the publisher, except in the case of brief quotations embodied in critical reviews and certain other non-commercial uses permitted by copyright law.

Copyright © Jamie C. Rider 2024.

Disclaimer

This book is an independent and unauthorized biography of Ina Garten, created without the involvement, endorsement, or approval of Ina Garten, the Food Network, or any of their associated entities. The content presented herein has been compiled from publicly accessible sources, and reflects the author's personal interpretation, analysis, and perspective on Ina Garten's life and career.

While every effort has been made to provide accurate and well-researched information, this biography does not claim to possess insider knowledge or include firsthand contributions from Ina Garten herself. The author has made every attempt to ensure the facts presented are reliable, but readers should be aware that some details may be subject to interpretation or may not have been directly confirmed by Ina Garten or her team.

This book is meant to celebrate Ina Garten's contributions to the culinary arts and the joy she has brought to her audience through her cookbooks, television appearances, and social media presence, without any formal association with her or her official brand.

Table of Contents

1. The Spark of a Culinary Passion 5
2. The Leap from Policy to Pastry 11
3. Crafting a Culinary Haven 17
4. Embracing the Art of Cooking 24
5. The Barefoot Contessa Takes the Spotlight ... 31
6. The Essence of Ina Garten's Culinary Philosophy 39
7. The Recipe for a Lasting Partnership 46
8. Crafting a Legacy: Ina Garten's Brand Evolution 53
9. Ina's Kitchen: A Sanctuary of Culinary Connection 60
10. A Legacy of Flavor, Comfort, and Connection 66
11. Overcoming Adversity and Achieving Success 72
12. The Heart of Ina's Success: A Network of Love and Collaboration 78
13. Thriving in a Modern Culinary Landscape 85
14. Epilogue 92

Chapter 1

The Spark of a Culinary Passion

A Childhood Rooted in Curiosity and Values

Ina Rosenberg's story begins on February 2, 1948, in the lively, culturally rich neighborhood of Brooklyn, New York. Born to Charles and Florence Rosenberg, Ina grew up in an environment that valued education, hard work, and intellectual curiosity. These formative values would later shape her life, both personally and professionally. Florence, a dietitian, and Charles, a respected surgeon, instilled in their daughter a deep respect for health, well-being, and knowledge. The Rosenbergs' home was always full of conversation, often revolving around food, nutrition, and medical care, but Ina's early exposure to food wasn't framed by a desire to become a culinary expert.

While her parents' professions were deeply entwined with the science of nutrition and the art of preparing wholesome meals, Ina's mother, Florence, had a particular sentiment about food—she wanted Ina to focus on academics and steer clear of the kitchen. "Stay out of the kitchen," Florence would say, directing Ina's attention toward her studies rather than the culinary world that seemed to captivate so many others. However, in hindsight, the kitchen was never far from Ina's consciousness, and though her mother's skills as a cook were never fully appreciated at the time, they undoubtedly laid the foundation for the culinary journey that would follow.

A Student with Hidden Interests

Despite being raised in a family where food and health played a central role, Ina's childhood and teenage years were marked by a natural inclination toward academics. She excelled in science and math—disciplines she would later describe as crucial to the way she approached recipe development. Ina found more excitement in books, school projects, and extracurricular activities than in experimenting with ingredients in the kitchen. Still, the world of food was always somewhere in the back of her mind, especially as she became increasingly aware of the role food played in connecting people, forging relationships, and fostering community.

Though her early academic success set her on a traditional path, a pivotal encounter would steer her life in an entirely different direction. During a visit to Dartmouth College to see her brother, Ina met Jeffrey Garten, a charismatic and ambitious young man who shared her intellectual curiosity but also had a deep love for food. Jeffrey's passion for gastronomy would soon ignite Ina's own interests and spark the beginning of a profound transformation in her life. His enthusiastic support of her pursuits, combined with his own admiration for food, laid the foundation for a future where culinary artistry would become as much a part of Ina's identity as her academic achievements.

A Life Shift: From Academia to Cooking

In 1968, at the age of 20, Ina married Jeffrey, and their journey together marked the beginning of a major shift in her life. While Jeffrey's career took him through military service and later academia and finance, Ina followed him to various locations, including Fort Bragg, North Carolina. It was here, far removed from the world of spreadsheets and textbooks, that Ina's culinary journey began to take shape.

With a copy of Julia Child's *Mastering the Art of French Cooking* in hand, Ina began experimenting in the kitchen, guided by a sense of adventure and an emerging passion for food. Cooking, initially a way to nurture and delight Jeffrey, became a creative outlet for Ina. Though her early meals were far from flawless, they sparked a sense of satisfaction and creativity that would grow into something much larger. For Ina, cooking became a means of expression, a way to connect with others, and a tool for offering comfort—a theme that would continue to define her career in the years to come.

Hospitality and the Art of Entertaining

Ina's upbringing, steeped in the importance of food and family, naturally led her to develop an appreciation for hospitality. She learned that it wasn't about grand displays or gourmet feasts, but about creating an atmosphere where people felt welcome, comfortable, and cared for. Whether hosting family gatherings or making guests feel at home, Ina's sense of hospitality was grounded in making others feel special. These early experiences, rooted in the art of entertaining, would prove invaluable as her career progressed.

As Ina's culinary experiments flourished, she began to realize that food wasn't just about sustenance—it was about connection. The simple act of sharing a meal with friends or family had the power to bring people together, break down barriers, and create lasting memories. Ina's love for food, born from curiosity and nurtured through the support of her family and Jeffrey, would eventually lead her to a career in the culinary world—a career that blended creativity, warmth, and hospitality into a lasting legacy.

The Beginning of a Transformative Journey

Ina Rosenberg's path from a bright, academically inclined girl in Brooklyn to a woman whose name would be synonymous with culinary expertise and hospitality was just beginning. Though her early experiments with food were small, her curiosity was boundless, and her journey into the world of cooking was already set in motion. Little did she know that her experiments with French cooking, her growing interest in making others feel welcome, and her passion for food would one day propel her into the culinary stardom she would come to embrace.

The spark of her culinary passion had been ignited, and with the unwavering support of Jeffrey and the nurturing values of her upbringing, Ina was ready to embark on a journey that would take her from the world of academia to the world of soufflés, from the quiet kitchen in Fort Bragg to the kitchens of renowned chefs and television screens.

Chapter 2

The Leap from Policy to Pastry

A Journey Steeped in Government and Strategy

After completing her MBA, Ina Garten embarked on a professional path that seemed far removed from the world of food and flavors. In the early 1970s, she secured a position at the White House Office of Management and Budget (OMB), where she played a key role in shaping nuclear energy policy under both Presidents Gerald Ford and Jimmy Carter. For almost a decade, Ina thrived in the high-stakes environment of government policy, where her analytical skills, sharp intellect, and composed demeanor became her hallmark.

Despite the success she found in this demanding role, Ina began to feel a growing sense of dissatisfaction. The long hours and complex policy work, while intellectually stimulating, were draining. She began to wonder if this path was truly hers to follow, or if it was simply the product of external pressures and expectations. In the high-pressure world of public service, Ina started to crave something more—a life that aligned more closely with her passions and allowed for personal expression.

Weekends of Culinary Reprieve

While her weekdays were filled with memos, meetings, and policy briefs, Ina found an escape in the weekends. She began retreating into her kitchen, where she found peace in the process of cooking. For Ina, the act of preparing meals wasn't just about food—it was a form of creative expression, a chance to unwind and engage in something deeply personal. Her weekends became a sanctuary, where she could experiment with new recipes, explore different flavors, and share her creations with friends.

In the evenings, Ina would host dinner parties for colleagues and friends, turning her home into a welcoming space for lively conversation and delicious food. These intimate gatherings became a canvas for Ina to showcase her culinary skills and innate hospitality. While her weekdays were spent navigating bureaucratic complexities, the weekends allowed her to indulge in the art of entertaining, where she could weave connections and offer a sense of warmth and community that contrasted with the cold, analytical nature of her day job.

The Catalyst for Change

In the late 1970s, as Ina settled into her routine of policy work by day and cooking by night, something happened that would change her life forever. One day, she came across an advertisement in *The New York Times* for a small specialty food shop for sale in East Hampton, New York. The idea of running a food business intrigued her, even though she had no experience in the industry. What caught her eye wasn't just the store itself, but the possibility of doing something completely different—something that was entirely her own.

Jeffrey, always supportive of Ina's ventures and dreams, encouraged her to take the plunge. "Why not?" he said, urging her to follow her heart. Despite the uncertainty of leaving a secure government position, Ina found herself drawn to the idea of starting something new. She began to see it not just as a business opportunity, but as a way to combine her love for food, hospitality, and creativity—elements that had always been a part of her but had been pushed aside in the world of politics.

Trading Suits for Aprons

In 1978, Ina made a decision that would completely reshape her life. Alongside Jeffrey, she drove to East Hampton to visit the shop, Barefoot Contessa. The store, though modest in size and somewhat outdated in design, immediately captured Ina's imagination. It wasn't the most glamorous or state-of-the-art establishment, but it held potential. It was warm and unpretentious, much like the name itself—a nod to a 1954 film featuring Ava Gardner. Ina saw a vision of a store that could serve high-quality food without the pretension often associated with gourmet dining.

After a quick and decisive negotiation, Ina made the life-changing decision to purchase the store. She left her stable government job, traded in her office suits for aprons, and transitioned from writing policy papers to crafting recipes. It was a leap into the unknown, but one that felt right in her heart. Ina was ready to step into a world that was far more uncertain but also far more fulfilling.

From the White House to the Kitchen

The early days of owning Barefoot Contessa were a whirlwind. Ina had no formal training in business or the culinary world, but she dove in headfirst, learning everything on the job. She taught herself everything from inventory management to customer service, relying on her organizational skills and passion for good food to guide her. Though the work was exhausting, it was also deeply rewarding.

Ina's transition from government policy to running a food store was about much more than a change in career. It was about rediscovering herself and aligning her daily work with her true passions. No longer confined to a desk, drafting energy policies and budget reports, Ina found a new sense of purpose in the kitchen. The satisfaction of feeding people, building relationships through shared meals, and creating something that was truly hers gave her a sense of fulfillment that her political career never had.

The move from office suits to aprons was not just a change in wardrobe—it was a symbolic shift from a life of calculations and politics to one of creativity and hospitality. Ina wasn't just transitioning to a new career; she was embracing a new way of life, one that aligned more closely with her values and aspirations.

A New Chapter Begins

Ina Garten's leap from politics to pastries wasn't just about a career change—it was a profound transformation. The skills she had honed in the White House, her ability to stay calm under pressure and solve complex problems, translated well into running a small business. But more importantly, this bold decision marked the beginning of a new chapter in Ina's life, one that would ultimately redefine her identity. The years of policy analysis and bureaucratic work were behind her, replaced by the joy of creating food, sharing meals, and fostering community.

Barefoot Contessa, the store that would come to symbolize Ina's culinary career, marked the start of a journey that would not only change her life but also leave a lasting legacy in the world of food and hospitality. Ina had found her calling—not in the corridors of government, but in the warmth of the kitchen, where creativity, connection, and authenticity could flourish.

Chapter 3

Crafting a Culinary Haven

A Bold Leap into the Unknown

In 1978, Ina Garten faced a pivotal moment in her life, one that would set her on a path that veered far from the world of policy and public service. After years of working in the White House Office of Management and Budget, Ina had grown restless, yearning for something more fulfilling, something that would tap into her creativity and passion. It was during a weekend getaway in East Hampton, New York, that Ina happened upon an intriguing advertisement in *The New York Times*. The ad was for a small specialty food store for sale, named **Barefoot Contessa**.

The name, taken from a 1954 film starring Ava Gardner, immediately captured Ina's imagination. Though the store was small and modest, it had a reputation for offering high-quality, gourmet products, beloved by locals. Ina, without any formal experience in retail or running a food business, was intrigued by the possibilities. She recalled later, "I thought, if this doesn't work, I'll just do something else."

Encouraged by Jeffrey, her supportive husband, Ina made the life-changing decision to take the plunge and buy the store. The world of policy and budgets was left behind, and a new adventure was about to unfold.

A Space to Create

Barefoot Contessa was more than just a specialty store—it was an idea waiting to blossom. Upon purchasing the business, Ina inherited a loyal base of customers and a small, dedicated team. The store's inventory consisted of high-end cheeses, baked goods, and other gourmet treats. However, Ina quickly saw that there was potential to offer more—she envisioned a space where food wasn't just about fine ingredients, but about creating connections and bringing people together through the joy of eating.

Ina began to use the store as a canvas for her own culinary vision, curating fresh, simple, and delicious products. Her love of cooking and hosting blossomed as she carefully selected new recipes and food items that reflected her philosophy of effortless elegance. **Barefoot Contessa** became known not only for its high-quality food, but also for the warm and inviting atmosphere Ina cultivated. Customers felt at home, often stopping by not only for groceries, but for Ina's welcoming smile and advice on how to throw the perfect dinner party.

Learning on the Job

The early days of running **Barefoot Contessa** were a whirlwind of excitement, exhaustion, and steep learning curves. Ina quickly found that owning a food business was no small feat. She juggled multiple roles—buyer, chef, marketer, and manager—all at once. With no formal training in retail or culinary entrepreneurship, she relied on intuition, creativity, and her own relentless drive.

Ina devoted countless hours to perfecting recipes, sourcing the best ingredients, and forming strong relationships with local suppliers. Despite the challenges, she found joy in every aspect of the business. The work was exhausting—18-hour days became the norm—but the satisfaction of seeing her customers' reactions to her food made it all worthwhile. Over time, these experiences helped Ina hone her business skills and expand her culinary expertise.

A Heartfelt Connection with the Community

As Ina poured her energy into **Barefoot Contessa**, the store evolved into a true community hub. People came from near and far—not just for the food, but for the warmth and hospitality that Ina so naturally offered. Her roasted chicken became legendary, her soups heartwarming, and her desserts nothing short of decadent. More than just food, Ina's offerings became symbols of comfort, joy, and connection.

The store was a place where conversations flowed as easily as the coffee, where locals and weekend visitors could relax, enjoy good food, and exchange stories. Ina's role as a host and creator was about more than business—it was about building relationships, making people feel welcome, and sharing the simple pleasures of life. This sense of community and belonging became a hallmark of **Barefoot Contessa**, and it was Ina's ability to connect with people on a personal level that made the store so special.

The Vision Expands

As **Barefoot Contessa** flourished, Ina began to feel a new calling—a desire to share her love for cooking and entertaining with a wider audience. She envisioned a platform that would allow her to inspire others to embrace the joy of cooking, creating memorable meals, and connecting with loved ones around the table.

Ina's passion for food and hospitality had always been personal, but as the store grew, she realized it was time to take her vision beyond the confines of East Hampton. She didn't know exactly how, but she was certain that **Barefoot Contessa** was just the beginning of something much bigger. The seeds of a new chapter were planted, one that would take her from a small store owner to a celebrated culinary personality.

A Bold New Direction

In 1996, after nearly two decades of nurturing **Barefoot Contessa**, Ina made another bold decision: she sold the store. The sale marked the end of one chapter and the beginning of another. With the store behind her, Ina turned her focus toward the next phase of her career—writing a cookbook that would reflect her signature cooking style, one that combined simplicity with elegance.

The success of **Barefoot Contessa** had not only been about selling food—it had been about creating an experience, about making people feel good and inspiring them to live well. Ina's philosophy of food as a means of connection, comfort, and celebration resonated with her customers and became the foundation of her enduring legacy.

Building a Legacy

Ina Garten's journey with **Barefoot Contessa** transformed her from a novice entrepreneur to a culinary icon. Through her store, she created a space that celebrated simple, delicious food, beautiful hospitality, and the joy of sharing meals with others. Her success wasn't measured solely by the number of products sold, but by the relationships she built, the community she fostered, and the way she inspired people to live more fully through the act of cooking.

The story of **Barefoot Contessa** is not just the story of a food store—it's a story of passion, hard work, and a desire to bring joy to others. It was the foundation upon which Ina would build a career that would eventually reach millions of people, inspiring them to create their own moments of joy in the kitchen and at the table. The legacy of **Barefoot Contessa** is a testament to the power of following your heart, trusting your instincts, and taking a leap of faith when the opportunity arises.

Chapter 4

Embracing the Art of Cooking

A New Direction on the Horizon

By the late 1990s, Ina Garten had reached another defining moment in her career. After nearly two decades of running **Barefoot Contessa**, a business she had nurtured with love and dedication, she found herself standing at the crossroads of what to do next. She had achieved success on her own terms, but she wasn't ready to rest. Her heart yearned for something more—a broader way to share her deep passion for cooking, entertaining, and the joy of creating meals that brought people together.

While some might have chosen to take a break after the sale of **Barefoot Contessa**, Ina's curiosity and drive pushed her toward a new challenge: sharing her culinary wisdom with the world. The idea that would propel her into her next chapter was simple yet powerful—a cookbook. It would encapsulate all that she had learned over the years, transforming her experiences as a cook, host, and business owner into a series of recipes and stories that could inspire others to cook with confidence and delight.

Crafting the Cookbook

Approaching the task of writing her first cookbook, Ina threw herself into the process with the same rigor and attention to detail that had shaped her earlier success. Though she had no formal background in publishing or food writing, Ina relied on her instincts as a cook and host. She knew what her customers loved from her years of owning **Barefoot Contessa**, and she believed those same tastes could resonate with a larger audience. The recipes she envisioned would not only need to be delicious but also accessible, reliable, and full of warmth.

Ina spent countless hours testing recipes in her home kitchen, perfecting each dish to reflect her signature style—simple, fresh, and elegant. She was meticulous, refining her creations until they were not only foolproof but also designed to inspire. Whether it was her famous roast chicken or her rich, indulgent brownies, every recipe was intended to show home cooks that they, too, could make impressive meals without feeling overwhelmed.

Overcoming the Hurdles

While the process of writing a cookbook was exhilarating, it was also filled with challenges. Ina had to learn how to transform her intuitive cooking style into clear, step-by-step instructions that could be followed by anyone. She struggled with doubts about whether her recipes, honed over years of personal experience, would translate to a wider audience. Would anyone outside of East Hampton connect with her cooking? Could she truly reach people across the country—and beyond—through the pages of a book?

But Ina's belief in her vision grew stronger with each round of feedback from friends and family. Their excitement and enthusiasm reinforced her confidence, proving that there was something special about her approach to cooking. Jeffrey, always her rock, was there every step of the way, offering encouragement and praise, pushing her to keep moving forward despite the hurdles.

The Launch of a Culinary Legacy

In 1999, **The Barefoot Contessa Cookbook** was finally published, marking the beginning of a new era in Ina Garten's career. The book was met with immediate acclaim, quickly becoming a bestseller. Its blend of stunning photography, approachable recipes, and Ina's warm, conversational tone made it feel like an intimate invitation into her kitchen. Readers were drawn not just to the recipes but to the personality that shone through each page. Ina wasn't just offering dishes to recreate—she was inviting people to embrace the art of cooking with a sense of ease and joy.

The success of the cookbook was overwhelming. Critics praised its simplicity and reliability, while home cooks marveled at how easy it was to follow Ina's recipes and achieve consistently delicious results. The book tapped into a growing desire for stress-free, flavorful cooking, capturing a moment in time when people were eager for something real and uncomplicated in the kitchen.

A Signature Approach to Cooking

With the publication of her first cookbook, Ina Garten established herself as a culinary voice to be reckoned with. Her signature approach was a blend of accessibility and elegance—recipes that felt elevated yet completely within reach for the average cook. Ina believed that cooking should be a joyful experience, not a source of stress. Her recipes were designed to empower home cooks, helping them feel confident and capable in the kitchen.

But it wasn't just about the food. Ina's personality and unique perspective on cooking made her stand out in the crowded world of cookbooks. Her humor, warmth, and straightforward advice created a genuine connection with readers. Ina didn't just teach people how to prepare meals; she encouraged them to embrace the process, to feel at ease, and to have fun while cooking.

Cultivating a Growing Community

The success of **The Barefoot Contessa Cookbook** brought with it something Ina hadn't anticipated—a growing, passionate community of fans. She began receiving letters from people across the world, sharing stories of how her recipes had become part of their family traditions. These messages were a revelation to Ina, confirming that her work had touched others in meaningful ways.

Her cookbook was no longer just a collection of recipes; it had become a way for Ina to build deeper connections with her readers. It reinforced her belief that food had the power to bring people together, to create lasting memories, and to make everyday moments extraordinary.

Cooking with Confidence: Ina's Philosophy

The success of **The Barefoot Contessa Cookbook** was a testament to Ina's core belief: cooking should be about joy, not perfection. Her approach wasn't about following rigid rules or trying to impress others—it was about creating meals that felt authentic and meaningful. Ina's emphasis on using fresh ingredients, her focus on simple yet elegant preparation, and her ability to make the cooking process feel approachable all helped readers embrace cooking as an act of self-expression and care.

For Ina, this was more than just a cookbook—it was a philosophy. Cooking was about confidence, creativity, and the freedom to enjoy the process without fear of failure. Ina's work helped readers understand that anyone, regardless of experience or skill level, could cook delicious meals that would delight their families and friends.

A Launchpad for the Future

With her first cookbook, Ina Garten set the stage for what would become a groundbreaking career. She had gone from a small-town store owner to a culinary icon, and her cookbook marked the beginning of her broader influence on the world of food. But the journey didn't end there—this was only the start.

The cookbook opened doors to new opportunities and wider recognition. Ina's influence grew beyond the pages of a single book, laying the groundwork for more cookbooks, television appearances, and a continued presence in the culinary world. Her journey had come full circle—from a small food shop in East Hampton to a celebrated figure in the global culinary community.

Through **The Barefoot Contessa Cookbook**, Ina had done more than share her recipes—she had created a legacy, one rooted in the belief that anyone could cook with confidence, and that the kitchen was a place for creativity, connection, and joy.

Chapter 5

The Barefoot Contessa Takes the Spotlight

A New Stage for Ina

In the early 2000s, Ina Garten was already basking in the success of her bestselling cookbooks, when a new, unexpected opportunity arose. Food Network, the popular channel known for its culinary programming, reached out to her with an offer to host her own cooking show. At first, Ina was hesitant. She had always been a private person, enjoying the quiet serenity of her life in East Hampton. The idea of becoming a television personality did not initially appeal to her. She was more comfortable in her home kitchen, with a small circle of friends and family.

However, after much consideration and several conversations with the network, Ina was persuaded by the potential to share her love for cooking with an even wider audience. What intrigued her most was the promise that the show would stay true to her authentic style. It would reflect her approach to food and entertaining—simple, elegant, and centered on the joy of cooking. After agreeing to the proposal, Ina Garten embarked on a new adventure: the creation of **Barefoot Contessa**, the television show.

Setting the Scene

Ina's vision for **Barefoot Contessa** was far from conventional. Unlike many cooking shows filmed in sterile, impersonal studio kitchens, Ina insisted that her show be filmed in her actual home. She felt it was crucial for the show to capture the essence of her life and the atmosphere she had cultivated in her East Hampton kitchen. Her space, filled with natural light and cozy charm, became as much a part of the show as the recipes themselves.

This intimate setting helped establish the tone for the program: approachable, warm, and authentic. Viewers felt as though they were right there with Ina in her kitchen, learning from a friend who was passionate about cooking and sharing that enthusiasm with them. The **Barefoot Contessa** show debuted in 2002, and from the start, it was clear that this was no ordinary cooking program.

The Secret to Ina's Appeal

What truly set Ina apart from other celebrity chefs on television was her unique blend of elegance and relatability. While other cooking personalities often relied on flashy, over-the-top presentations, Ina's charm lay in her simplicity. She wasn't interested in playing to the camera with dramatic flourishes or exaggerated theatrics. Instead, her approach was calm, gentle, and inviting. With her soothing voice, graceful demeanor, and genuine passion for food, Ina made viewers feel as if they were in the presence of an old friend.

Her recipes were the cornerstone of the show's success. They were simple, yet flavorful, and relied on a few high-quality ingredients rather than complicated techniques. Dishes like her signature roast chicken or her indulgent chocolate ganache cake became iconic—aspirational, yet entirely achievable for home cooks. Ina's philosophy was clear: delicious food could be made without stress or complexity.

A Glimpse Into Her Life

In addition to cooking, **Barefoot Contessa** gave viewers a glimpse into Ina's life beyond the kitchen. Regular appearances by Jeffrey, her husband, along with snippets of their East Hampton garden, social gatherings, and casual entertaining, offered a deeper sense of who Ina was. The show wasn't just about food; it was about creating an experience, both for the people in her life and for those watching at home.

This personal touch made the show feel authentic. Ina wasn't just presenting recipes; she was showing how food was woven into the fabric of her life. Whether she was hosting a casual dinner party or preparing a special meal for friends, the focus was on making those moments meaningful and enjoyable—not perfect. Ina's relaxed, no-fuss style of entertaining was part of the show's allure, as viewers were invited not only to recreate the dishes but also to embrace Ina's laid-back approach to life.

Behind the Camera

Though **Barefoot Contessa** had the relaxed vibe of a home-cooked meal shared with friends, the reality behind the scenes was a bit more meticulous. Ina was known for being a perfectionist, working closely with her production team to ensure every recipe, shot, and segment met her high standards. She was involved in every aspect of the show, from the food to the lighting, to the music that accompanied each episode.

"I want people to feel confident when they cook my recipes," Ina explained. "That means everything has to work perfectly." This attention to detail was a key element in the show's success, and Ina's dedication to excellence helped ensure that **Barefoot Contessa** stood out as a culinary program that didn't just entertain—it educated and inspired.

A Genuine Connection

Ina's approachable style struck a chord with viewers of all backgrounds and skill levels. The show became a platform for Ina to connect with her audience on a deeper level, as fans began to share their own experiences with her recipes. Letters poured in from people who had used her dishes to host dinner parties, create family traditions, or even to overcome their fear of cooking. Many fans credited Ina with teaching them more than just how to cook—she showed them how to enjoy life's simple pleasures.

Whether she was demonstrating how to prepare a simple weeknight meal or offering tips for setting an elegant table, Ina's message was clear: cooking should be fun, not stressful. Her warmth and sincerity resonated with viewers, making them feel empowered and capable in the kitchen. She wasn't just teaching them how to follow recipes; she was teaching them how to approach cooking with confidence and creativity.

The Contessa Effect

Over time, **Barefoot Contessa** became one of Food Network's most beloved programs, winning multiple awards and earning a dedicated following. Ina's influence grew beyond the television screen, with her recipes inspiring a shift in home cooking culture. Viewers were encouraged to embrace fresh ingredients, simple preparation, and the joy of creating meals without fuss.

Ina's trademark phrases—such as "How easy is that?" and "Store-bought is fine"—became part of the cultural lexicon, reflecting her laid-back yet effective approach to cooking. Her influence extended beyond the kitchen, as she became a trusted figure in the world of food, entertaining, and hospitality. She showed that meals didn't need to be overly complex or intimidating to be special.

A Platform for Ina's Passion

For Ina Garten, **Barefoot Contessa** was more than just a cooking show. It was an opportunity to share her passion for food, hospitality, and the joys of simple living with a broader audience. Through the show, she empowered millions of viewers to embrace their kitchens, not as a place of stress, but as a space for creativity, connection, and joy.

What made **Barefoot Contessa** so successful was Ina's unwavering authenticity. She didn't just appear on television to promote herself or her brand; she was there to share her love of food, family, and entertaining in a way that felt genuine and unpretentious. Ina Garten didn't just teach people how to cook; she invited them into her world, where cooking was always a celebration of life's simplest and most meaningful moments.

As **Barefoot Contessa** soared in popularity, Ina remained grounded in her original vision. Her television career wasn't about fame or fortune—it was about connecting with people, teaching them to cook with confidence, and inspiring them to gather around the table with loved ones. Through her authenticity and warmth, Ina Garten not only transformed how people cook and entertain; she changed how they think about food and hospitality.

Chapter 6

The Essence of Ina Garten's Culinary Philosophy

The Soul of Cooking

Ina Garten's approach to food and hospitality is not simply a set of techniques—it is a philosophy that underscores the beauty of simplicity, quality, and the joy of sharing meals with others. For Ina, cooking is not just a task to complete; it's a means to create meaningful experiences that nourish both the body and soul. Whether she's preparing a meal for her closest friends or hosting a festive gathering, her philosophy centers around bringing people together through the pleasures of good food and shared moments.

Elegance in Simplicity

One of Ina Garten's most notable qualities is her ability to simplify seemingly complex culinary ideas. She believes that exceptional food doesn't require elaborate techniques or exotic ingredients. As Ina often says:

"When you start with really good ingredients, you don't need to do much to make them taste delicious."

This simple yet profound belief is reflected in every dish she prepares. From perfectly roasted chicken to the simplest of salads, Ina's recipes focus on fresh, high-quality ingredients that need little adornment to shine. Her cooking style emphasizes that less is often more, and that elegance can be found in the most straightforward preparations. Whether for a weeknight dinner or a special celebration, Ina's recipes aim to deliver big flavors with minimal fuss.

A Deep Love for Fresh, Seasonal Ingredients

Ina's love for fresh ingredients is at the core of her culinary philosophy, and it traces back to her time in Paris. There, she was captivated by the city's bustling markets and the seasonal dishes that showcased the freshest produce. This experience left a lasting impression on her, and she carried that philosophy back to East Hampton, where she now sources her ingredients from local farmers and grows many of her own herbs and vegetables.

In Ina's kitchen, the focus is always on what's in season, as she believes that food tastes best when it is at its peak. By cooking with ingredients that are naturally ripe and full of flavor, Ina's dishes honor the earth's cycles and encourage home cooks to explore what's fresh and available. She advocates for creating meals around what nature offers, emphasizing that there's no need to overcomplicate things when ingredients speak for themselves.

Entertaining with Heart

For Ina, entertaining is not about achieving perfection or impressing guests with complicated dishes. Instead, it is about making meaningful connections with loved ones and creating a welcoming atmosphere where everyone feels comfortable. She stresses the importance of enjoying the moment rather than focusing on perfection in the kitchen.

Ina's most famous mantra when it comes to entertaining is: "Make it ahead." This advice allows hosts to prepare dishes in advance, freeing them to spend time with their guests rather than being tethered to the stove. Ina believes that the true success of any gathering lies in the experience shared, not in the intricacies of the menu. As she puts it, "People won't remember what you cooked, but they will remember how you made them feel."

Her approach to hospitality also extends to the little touches that elevate a gathering: a beautifully set table, soft background music, and a warm atmosphere. These details, she believes, are what make an event memorable and meaningful, and they show guests that they are truly valued.

Encouraging Confidence in the Kitchen

At the heart of Ina Garten's cooking philosophy is the desire to empower others to cook with confidence. She designs her recipes to be accessible, foolproof, and adaptable, so that anyone—from beginners to seasoned home cooks—can approach them with ease. Her step-by-step instructions and careful testing ensure that each recipe is reliable, allowing cooks to feel secure in their ability to recreate the dishes.

Ina also emphasizes the importance of flexibility in the kitchen. While she provides clear instructions, she encourages cooks to make adjustments based on their own preferences or what they have on hand. Her philosophy is that cooking should be enjoyable and intuitive, not rigid or stressful. Whether you're substituting an ingredient or improvising a recipe, Ina assures her audience that it's okay to make the dish your own.

The Practical Approach: "Store-Bought is Fine"

One of Ina's most widely recognized catchphrases is "Store-bought is fine," which epitomizes her practical and no-pressure approach to cooking. While she advocates for fresh, homemade dishes whenever possible, she also acknowledges the realities of modern life. Ina understands that sometimes there isn't enough time to make everything from scratch, and that's okay. Whether it's a jar of good-quality marinara sauce or a store-bought cake, Ina believes that shortcuts, when used thoughtfully, can enhance the overall experience without compromising on taste or enjoyment.

Her fans appreciate this permission to take a more relaxed approach to cooking, and they are drawn to her down-to-earth, practical style. It's not about perfection—it's about finding balance and joy in the process of cooking and entertaining.

Hospitality as an Act of Love

Central to Ina's cooking philosophy is the idea that food is a powerful tool for showing love and care. She views both cooking and entertaining as acts of generosity—gestures that demonstrate how much you value the people you share your meals with. Her belief in hospitality goes beyond providing nourishment; it's about creating an environment where people feel welcomed, appreciated, and cherished.

Ina's warmth and approachability have made her a beloved figure not only in the culinary world but also for anyone who aspires to create a joyful, hospitable home. She serves as a role model for those who wish to cultivate a sense of generosity and warmth in their own kitchens, proving that the best meals are those shared with love.

A Philosophy That Transcends Trends

What makes Ina Garten's culinary philosophy so enduring is that it is rooted in timeless principles: simplicity, quality, and the joy of togetherness. While food trends may come and go, Ina's approach remains steadfast, offering a sense of reliability and comfort in an ever-evolving culinary landscape. Her belief that good food doesn't need to be complicated and that meals should be enjoyed, not stressed over, has resonated with countless home cooks over the years.

Through her philosophy, Ina has done more than just teach people how to cook; she has inspired them to embrace the beauty of the table, to savor life's simplest moments, and to cherish the bonds created through shared meals. Ina Garten has reshaped the way we think about food and hospitality, encouraging us to cook with confidence, entertain with ease, and, above all, enjoy the pleasures of a life well-lived.

Chapter 7

The Recipe for a Lasting Partnership

A Timeless Love Story

At the very heart of Ina Garten's personal and professional life lies her enduring partnership with her husband, Jeffrey Garten. Their relationship, built on mutual respect, admiration, and a shared sense of humor, has been a key source of stability and joy for Ina, both personally and in her career. Together, they have created a love story that has captured the hearts of many and continues to inspire those who believe in the power of partnership and support in a lasting relationship.

The Sweet Beginning

Ina and Jeffrey's journey began in the late 1960s, when Ina visited her brother at Dartmouth College, where Jeffrey was a student. It was, as Jeffrey likes to recall, love at first sight. He famously sent Ina a photograph of himself with a simple note that read, "You look like someone I'd like to know." That spontaneous gesture marked the start of their relationship, one filled with shared curiosity, adventure, and deep mutual admiration.

Their courtship blossomed through their shared intellectual curiosity and respect for one another's passions. Jeffrey, who saw in Ina the potential for greatness, was unwavering in his belief in her abilities. Ina, in turn, was drawn to Jeffrey's intellect, his kindness, and his deep sense of integrity. They married in 1968, beginning a journey that would not only unite their lives but also set the stage for many of the personal and professional milestones that would come.

The Pillar of Support

Throughout their marriage, Jeffrey has been an unwavering pillar of support for Ina. His encouragement played a crucial role when Ina made the bold decision to leave her stable government job and purchase the Barefoot Contessa, a specialty food store. He believed in her vision for the store, offering both practical advice and emotional support when she needed it most. His confidence in Ina's instincts gave her the courage to take risks and follow her entrepreneurial dreams.

Despite his own demanding career, which frequently took him away from home to teach at Yale University and work in international finance, their bond only grew stronger. Ina often speaks fondly of the handwritten notes Jeffrey would send her during his travels, and the weekends they spent together were always a source of joy and reconnection. His absence, paradoxically, only deepened their emotional connection, as both partners learned to appreciate the time they spent together even more.

Jeffrey: The Muse and the Taster

Jeffrey has become more than just a supportive husband—he has become a beloved figure in Ina's public life. From the pages of her cookbooks to her appearances on television, Jeffrey is frequently seen enjoying her meals with visible delight. His genuine appreciation for Ina's cooking and his playful critiques have made him an endearing presence, not only in her life but also in the hearts of her fans.

Ina often refers to Jeffrey as her muse. Many of the recipes she creates are inspired by him, including his all-time favorite dishes, such as her signature roast chicken or decadent chocolate cake. For Ina, cooking is not just about preparing a meal; it's about expressing her love through food. She pours her affection into the dishes she prepares for him, and the personal connection they share through food has resonated deeply with Ina's audience. It's a love story that is felt not just by the couple but by everyone who enjoys Ina's cooking.

The Balance Between Togetherness and Independence

One of the most remarkable aspects of Ina and Jeffrey's relationship is their ability to balance time together with time apart. Jeffrey's professional life required frequent travel, and while it was difficult at times, the couple found ways to stay connected. They both understood the importance of maintaining their individual passions and interests, which helped them lead fulfilling lives both independently and as a couple.

Ina has often spoken about how their separate pursuits enriched their relationship. She believes that maintaining independence is crucial for a healthy partnership, as it allows each person to grow individually while still supporting and nurturing the bond they share. Whether it was traveling to Paris for a romantic getaway or simply spending quiet evenings at their home in East Hampton, Ina and Jeffrey have always found ways to prioritize quality time together.

Jeffrey: The Bedrock of Her Success

Jeffrey's support has been a constant throughout Ina's professional journey. From her early days as a small business owner to becoming the renowned culinary icon she is today, Jeffrey's belief in her potential never wavered. He encouraged her to take bold risks, like writing her first cookbook and launching her television career. His unwavering faith in her abilities provided the emotional foundation Ina needed to navigate the challenges and uncertainties that came with her professional success.

In return, Ina has celebrated their relationship through her work. Many of her recipes and cookbooks are imbued with the essence of their life together, reflecting the love and experiences they have shared. Ina's work has become a way for her to honor their partnership and the support Jeffrey has given her, both personally and professionally. Their relationship, full of warmth and authenticity, has become an integral part of Ina's public persona, making them one of the most beloved couples in the culinary world.

The True Meaning of Love

The enduring partnership between Ina and Jeffrey serves as a model for many who seek to understand the power of love, mutual respect, and support in a relationship. Their story is a reminder that the best partnerships are built on trust, kindness, and shared joy. Whether it's savoring a simple meal together or navigating the complexities of a career, Ina and Jeffrey have shown that the key to a happy and fulfilling relationship is rooted in the small, everyday acts of love.

Their relationship has shaped not only Ina's personal life but also her professional narrative. Through their love, Ina has learned the value of laughter, shared moments, and creating a life that's not just about success, but about cherishing those who matter most. The lessons of their partnership—how to balance togetherness with independence, how to encourage and uplift one another, and how to find joy in the simplest of moments—are at the heart of Ina's philosophy on love, food, and life.

Together, Ina and Jeffrey have demonstrated that the recipe for a successful and fulfilling life is best enjoyed with someone you truly love, someone who supports your dreams, shares in your triumphs, and stands by you through every challenge.

Chapter 8

Crafting a Legacy: Ina Garten's Brand Evolution

From Local Entrepreneur to Global Icon

What started as a small specialty food store in East Hampton has blossomed into a culinary empire, propelling Ina Garten into the ranks of culinary legends. Her journey from humble beginnings as a local business owner to becoming an internationally recognized name is a story fueled by vision, authenticity, and an unyielding commitment to her audience. Ina's brand grew organically, nurtured by a genuine connection with her fans and a deep love for what she does. This chapter explores how Ina masterfully expanded her brand, using her cookbooks, television show, and thoughtful partnerships to build a timeless, relatable identity that resonates across generations.

The Written Word: A Tool for Connection

Ina's rise as a household name can largely be attributed to the success of her first cookbook, *The Barefoot Contessa Cookbook*. This breakthrough success made Ina realize that her gift wasn't just in creating delicious recipes but in connecting with her readers on a personal level. As she wrote each subsequent book, Ina's distinctive voice—warm, approachable, and supportive—became a defining characteristic of her brand. Her books were more than collections of recipes; they were invitations into Ina's world, offering not only simple and elegant meals but also practical advice that empowered readers to confidently entertain and cook at home.

Books like *Barefoot Contessa Parties!* and *Make It Ahead* proved to be game-changers in the world of culinary publishing. Whether she was offering solutions for hosting sophisticated dinner parties or providing practical weeknight meal ideas, Ina's titles resonated with a broad range of home cooks. Her ability to address real-life cooking needs with accessible yet elevated recipes made each book a bestseller and cemented her reputation as a culinary authority with a relatable touch.

Television Stardom: Creating Intimacy in the Kitchen

The launch of the *Barefoot Contessa* television show was a natural next step in the evolution of Ina's brand. The show gave her an opportunity to connect with an even wider audience, bringing her warm and inviting personality into homes across the country. Ina's calm and steady demeanor, paired with her easy-to-follow cooking techniques, made her show feel like a cozy visit with an old friend. Her television program was about more than just cooking—it was about creating an intimate experience for viewers, making them feel as though they were right there in her East Hampton kitchen, cooking along with her.

Unlike many of her peers in the food television world, Ina's show did not rely on flashy competitions or sensational drama. Instead, it focused on the beauty of simplicity, with Ina demonstrating step-by-step how to prepare comforting, flavorful meals. This commitment to authenticity became a defining characteristic of Ina's brand, and it helped her stand apart in a crowded and often chaotic television landscape. The success of the show was built on the trust she cultivated with her audience—viewers knew that with Ina, there would always be a delicious result, and a feeling of calm, no matter how complicated the dish might seem.

Thoughtful Collaborations: Expanding the Brand

As her brand continued to grow, Ina expanded beyond cookbooks and television into a carefully curated collection of collaborations and product lines. From pantry staples to cookware, every product that bore her name adhered to the same principles that guided her culinary philosophy: simplicity, quality, and elegance. Each product was designed to reflect Ina's commitment to creating the best possible experience for home cooks, whether they were preparing a weeknight meal or a lavish celebration.

One notable example of this was her line of Barefoot Contessa cake mixes. These mixes allowed home bakers to recreate Ina's signature desserts with ease, ensuring that anyone could experience the magic of her cooking, even if they were short on time. By offering these products, Ina ensured that her fans could enjoy a piece of her world, even without the time or ingredients to prepare everything from scratch. This ability to balance elegance with accessibility became a hallmark of her brand.

Authenticity and Trust: The Foundation of Ina's Brand

At the core of Ina Garten's success is her unwavering commitment to authenticity and trust. She has built her brand by staying true to her values and ensuring that every product, recipe, and partnership aligns with her personal beliefs. From the very beginning, Ina was selective about the products she chose to endorse, always turning down opportunities that did not align with her brand's ethos. She understood that her audience trusted her, and she valued that trust above all else.

Ina's refusal to compromise on quality and her steadfast dedication to providing reliable, practical cooking advice have made her brand synonymous with consistency. Fans know that when they follow an Ina Garten recipe, it will work, and that they'll be met with a delicious result. This reliability has kept her brand strong, even as trends in the food world have come and gone.

Embracing New Platforms: Reaching a New Generation

As the culinary world evolved with the advent of social media, Ina was quick to adapt while staying grounded in her original philosophy.

Platforms like Instagram gave her the opportunity to connect with a younger, tech-savvy audience, offering glimpses into her life, her cooking process, and her East Hampton home. Through carefully curated posts and behind-the-scenes moments, Ina was able to offer a more personal side of herself, allowing fans to see the woman behind the recipes they loved.

Her Instagram presence, often punctuated with her signature phrase, "How easy is that?", further reinforced her brand's core message of simplicity and accessibility. Ina's posts were not just about showcasing perfect meals; they were about creating a conversation, inviting her audience into her world and making them feel like part of her culinary journey. Her ability to connect with fans, old and new, through social media allowed her to extend her reach and solidify her place in the modern food landscape.

An Empire Built on Simplicity and Authenticity

Ina Garten's brand is a testament to the power of simplicity done exceptionally well. In an industry often dominated by fads and trends, Ina has stayed true to her core values of quality, elegance, and approachability. Her success lies not in overcomplicating things, but in doing what she loves—creating delicious, accessible recipes that bring people together—and doing it consistently. Ina's brand is rooted in authenticity and the belief that great food and the best moments in life are often the simplest.

Her ability to stay true to herself while evolving with the times has allowed her to build an empire that feels both timeless and relatable. From her cookbooks to her television show, from her product lines to her social media presence, Ina Garten has created a brand that feels like a trusted friend, always there to offer a delicious recipe, a warm word of encouragement, and a reminder that life's greatest joys are often found in the simplest moments shared with those we love.

Chapter 9

Ina's Kitchen: A Sanctuary of Culinary Connection

The Heartbeat of the Home

Ina Garten's kitchen is not just a space where meals are prepared—it is the very heart of her home, a sanctuary where her culinary philosophy comes to life. For Ina, cooking goes beyond the mere act of preparing food; it's about nurturing relationships, celebrating life's milestones, and creating a warm, welcoming atmosphere for everyone who enters. This chapter explores the true essence of Ina's kitchen, looking at how her approach to food, hospitality, and the emotional power of her recipes has transformed her kitchen into something far more profound than just a cooking space.

Simplicity Meets Elegance: Ina's Culinary Philosophy

The hallmark of Ina Garten's cooking is the elegant simplicity she brings to every dish. Whether she's preparing a comforting roast chicken or an indulgent lobster pot pie, the focus of Ina's recipes is always on using the finest, freshest ingredients and allowing them to speak for themselves. Her dishes are designed to be sophisticated yet uncomplicated, a perfect reflection of her belief that food should be approachable and refined without being intimidating.

Ina's cooking is rooted in the idea that anyone, regardless of their skill level, can create something truly delicious. She removes unnecessary complications from her recipes, ensuring that each dish is easy to follow and allows home cooks to shine. One of her most famous sayings, "If you can read, you can cook," encapsulates this approach, giving her fans the confidence to embrace their culinary skills and experiment in their own kitchens.

Iconic Dishes with Personal Significance

Certain dishes have become synonymous with Ina's name, and each of these recipes carries its own special story. Her perfect roast chicken, for example, is not only known for being a fail-safe dish but also for its personal connection to her family. Ina often shares that this was one of her husband Jeffrey's favorite meals, imbuing the dish with a sense of warmth and familiarity that resonates with her audience.

Other beloved recipes, like her infamous outrageous brownies and refreshing lemon bars, are staples in her culinary repertoire, evoking nostalgia and a sense of timelessness. These dishes go beyond being mere recipes; they are expressions of Ina's life, her tastes, and her experiences. Each one tells a story, inviting her followers to share in the joy and simplicity that Ina finds in the kitchen.

Cooking with the Purpose of Connection

At the core of Ina Garten's cooking philosophy is the notion of food as a bridge that connects people. Ina's recipes are created not just to nourish the body, but to bring people together, creating memorable moments around the table. She firmly believes that hosting should be a joyous occasion, free of stress, where the focus is on enjoying the company of guests rather than worrying about the complexity of the meal.

From her signature Sunday rib roast to a refreshing cosmopolitan cocktail, every recipe Ina shares is designed to foster a sense of warmth and hospitality. Ina often emphasizes that food is an expression of love, and the act of preparing and sharing a meal with loved ones is an invaluable way to show care and appreciation. For Ina, the true joy of cooking lies not in creating the most elaborate dishes, but in making people feel welcome, cherished, and nourished in both body and spirit.

The Power of Food to Connect Cultures

While Ina's cooking is rooted in American and French culinary traditions, her kitchen is a place where diverse global influences come together. From the Middle Eastern notes in her Israeli couscous salad to the Italian flavors in her beloved weeknight bolognese, Ina's recipes are a testament to her openness to the world's varied culinary traditions.

Ina's embrace of global flavors reflects her belief that food is a universal language. Just as it transcends borders, food has the power to unite people from different backgrounds, cultures, and experiences. Through her dishes, Ina fosters a deeper understanding of the richness that different cuisines bring, while celebrating the commonalities that bind us all— our shared love for delicious, home-cooked meals.

Ina's Kitchen as a Metaphor for Life

For many, Ina's kitchen symbolizes the ideal— an environment filled with warmth, creativity, and comfort. Through her food, her advice, and her gentle encouragement, Ina has inspired millions to transform their own kitchens into places where joy, inspiration, and togetherness thrive. Her kitchen isn't just a room in her home; it is a metaphor for how we should approach life itself—focusing on quality over quantity, simplicity over complexity, and connection over perfection.

Ina's philosophy is one that encourages embracing the joy in life's small moments, and her recipes are designed to reflect this mindset. The kitchen, in Ina's view, is a space where we can come together to share in the simple pleasures of food, laughter, and love. It's a place where creativity and tradition meet, and where each meal becomes an opportunity to make meaningful memories.

A Legacy Built on Flavor and Feeling

Ina Garten's kitchen is more than a culinary space—it is a reflection of her enduring legacy. Through her food, she has touched the lives of countless people, helping them to create memories with family and friends, and showing them that cooking can be a form of love. She has demystified the world of gourmet cooking, making it accessible to home cooks everywhere, and empowering them to embrace the joys of preparing and sharing meals.

Ina's influence extends beyond the recipes she creates—she has fostered a deeper appreciation for food as a way of connecting with others, a tool for building relationships, and a means of celebrating life's most treasured moments. Her kitchen is a testament to the magic that happens when great food is paired with great company. It is a space that invites us to step away from the chaos of the outside world and into a place of comfort, creativity, and togetherness.

Through her approach to cooking and hospitality, Ina Garten has not only created delicious dishes but has also created a way of life—one that encourages people to savor the moment, appreciate the simple joys of cooking, and share the love that comes with a meal prepared with care. Her kitchen, with its warmth and simplicity, is a true reflection of her legacy: a place where food becomes more than just nourishment, but a powerful means of connection and joy.

Chapter 10

A Legacy of Flavor, Comfort, and Connection

A Culinary Icon

Ina Garten's reach extends far beyond the confines of her kitchen, influencing countless individuals around the world. Her ability to redefine home cooking has empowered people to approach food with both confidence and excitement. Through her cookbooks, television shows, and public appearances, Ina has built a remarkable connection with her audience, solidifying her place as a cultural icon in the culinary world. She is more than a chef—she is a symbol of accessibility, warmth, and a reinvention of what it means to cook at home.

Transforming Home Cooking

Ina's work has revolutionized the way people view home cooking. What was once seen as a mundane or tedious task has been elevated into an art form that anyone can partake in. By emphasizing the importance of fresh, high-quality ingredients and simple yet elegant cooking techniques, she has shown that cooking at home can be both enjoyable and rewarding. Her approach encourages people to take pride in their kitchens, transforming everyday meals into moments of joy.

Ina's recipes are now staples in homes across the globe. From her herb-roasted turkey breast to her famous parmesan crisps and the elegant French apple tart, these dishes have come to embody both comfort and sophistication. By making gourmet cooking accessible, Ina has left a legacy that proves anyone, regardless of their cooking experience, can produce meals worthy of a fine dining experience. Her influence has made cooking feel attainable and, more importantly, fun, helping her audience discover the joy of creating meals from scratch.

Mentoring Through Media

Ina's presence on television, especially through her long-running show *Barefoot Contessa*, has made her a mentor to millions of viewers. Her calm and reassuring demeanor, combined with her approachable personality, has made her an inspiring figure for home cooks of all levels. With her signature catchphrase, "How easy is that?" Ina has shown that cooking doesn't need to be complicated to be rewarding, fostering a sense of empowerment in her audience.

Beyond her television appearances, Ina has successfully leveraged social media to connect with her fans in new and more personal ways. Her Instagram feed offers a mix of behind-the-scenes glimpses of her life, personal anecdotes, and, of course, mouthwatering dishes that embody the simplicity and elegance of her culinary style. Through these posts, she feels like a trusted friend, inviting her followers into her world and sharing some of her best-kept secrets. This personal connection has deepened her impact, making her a figure that is both relatable and aspirational.

A Powerful Influence on the Culinary Industry

Ina Garten's influence in the culinary world is profound and enduring. She has inspired a new generation of chefs, cookbook authors, and home cooks, setting a high standard for culinary storytelling. Through her cookbooks and television work, she has elevated the role of the home cook, proving that exceptional food doesn't have to come from a professional kitchen. Her focus on quality ingredients and simple preparation has paved the way for many aspiring chefs to embrace a similar philosophy in their own work.

Ina's unwavering commitment to quality and authenticity has earned her the respect of her peers. Chefs, food writers, and celebrities frequently cite her as an influence, acknowledging the impact she has had on how food is approached and appreciated in modern kitchens. Her signature style of simplicity, elegance, and approachability has become a blueprint for others to follow, raising the profile of the home cook and making cooking feel more inclusive.

A Cultural Touchstone

Ina Garten has transcended her role as a chef to become a true cultural phenomenon. Her popularity goes beyond her culinary expertise; it has captured the imaginations of millions drawn to her lifestyle, humor, and approachable philosophy. Ina's marriage to her husband, Jeffrey, has been a source of public affection, with their endearing relationship often celebrated in memes and pop culture references. The image of the couple—living a charming, cozy life in their East Hampton home—has become a symbol of domestic bliss, and their connection is admired by fans worldwide.

Ina's appeal spans across diverse demographics. Whether she's inspiring busy parents, young professionals, or aspiring cooks, her influence resonates with people from all walks of life. Her message—that great food and good company are at the heart of a fulfilling life—has universal appeal, reminding us all of the importance of simple pleasures and meaningful connections.

Recognition and Honors

Ina's exceptional contribution to the world of food has not gone unnoticed. Over the years, she has received numerous prestigious accolades, including Emmy Awards for her television work and James Beard Foundation Awards for her cookbooks. These honors reflect not only her culinary excellence but also her significant and lasting influence on American cooking and food culture.

These accolades are a testament to Ina's unwavering dedication to her craft, as well as her ability to create work that resonates deeply with audiences. Her influence has shaped the way cooking is approached, both at home and professionally, and these awards solidify her legacy as one of the most important culinary figures of her generation.

A Legacy of Culinary Connection

The legacy of Ina Garten is firmly rooted in her ability to bring people together through the simple act of cooking. Her recipes, her philosophy, and her personal warmth have created an enduring connection with her audience, inspiring countless people to embrace the joy of cooking and entertaining. Ina has proven that cooking is not just about feeding people—it is about creating lasting memories and meaningful moments.

Through her ability to blend simplicity with elegance, Ina has redefined modern cooking. Her approach is grounded in the belief that food should bring joy, not stress, and her influence will undoubtedly continue to inspire generations of home cooks to come. Ina's legacy shows that cooking is not just a skill—it is a way to connect, celebrate, and express love. Through her work, Ina has demonstrated that the best meals are often the simplest, and the best memories are made around a table, sharing food with those we care about most.

Chapter 11

Overcoming Adversity and Achieving Success

Ina Garten's rise to culinary fame has not been a smooth or straightforward journey. While it may seem like her success was inevitable, her story is rich with moments of doubt, setbacks, and obstacles that could have derailed her career. However, it is in overcoming these challenges that Ina has truly forged her path. This chapter explores the various hurdles she faced and how, through persistence and resilience, she transformed each challenge into a stepping stone toward her remarkable success.

Taking Bold Risks: A Leap into the Unknown

One of the most significant challenges Ina faced came early in her career when she made the bold decision to leave her stable job in government to pursue a career in food. At the time, Ina had no formal culinary training or any experience in business management. The idea of buying a small, struggling food store in East Hampton, which she would later rename

Barefoot Contessa, was a major risk. Ina herself admitted that she had never been in a management position before, let alone run her own business. Yet, despite the initial fear and uncertainty, her determination, innate understanding of flavors, and a deep passion for food helped her turn the business around. What started as a modest venture soon flourished into a thriving specialty food store, setting the foundation for what would later become Ina's empire.

The Struggles of Writing a Cookbook

Ina's journey as a cookbook author came with its own set of hurdles. When she first began working on *The Barefoot Contessa Cookbook*, she quickly realized that translating her instinctual cooking style into written recipes that others could follow was no easy feat. Ina's cooking has always been intuitive, built on years of personal experience and an innate sense of flavor. However, the challenge lay in making her dishes accessible and foolproof for a wide range of home cooks. Early drafts of the cookbook were rejected by her publisher, forcing Ina to reconsider her approach. She poured over every detail, refining and simplifying the recipes until they could be replicated with ease by anyone. After two years of hard work and revisions, *The Barefoot Contessa Cookbook* was published in 1999, and it was met with instant success, becoming a beloved classic that solidified Ina's place in the culinary world.

Maintaining Authenticity Amidst Growing Fame

As her career gained momentum, Ina found herself facing the pressures that come with fame. The demands on her time and energy grew, and with her newfound success, there were constant opportunities for her to expand her brand. However, Ina remained committed to staying true to her values. She was offered lucrative deals to mass-produce her products, but she turned them down, prioritizing quality over quantity. This decision was not without its critics, but Ina's unwavering commitment to maintaining the integrity of her brand paid off. Her decision to keep her work authentic and personal has been a key element of her enduring popularity. Ina knew that the core of her success lay in the trust and connection she had built with her audience, and she was unwilling to compromise that for the sake of rapid expansion.

Embracing the Digital Shift

With the rise of social media and digital platforms, Ina faced a new challenge: how to adapt to an ever-changing media landscape. Initially, she was hesitant to embrace platforms like Instagram, which were increasingly being used by chefs and food influencers to build their brands. However, Ina soon recognized the potential of these platforms to connect with her audience in a more intimate and personal way. Through her Instagram, she shared not just her recipes but glimpses of her life in East Hampton, offering a behind-the-scenes look at her culinary world. This new digital presence helped Ina maintain relevance in an industry that was rapidly shifting toward social media-driven marketing, allowing her to stay connected with her fans while continuing to promote her brand in a fresh and accessible way.

Personal Struggles and Strength

Ina's resilience is not limited to her professional challenges. Like many, she has faced personal hurdles that tested her strength and determination. One of the most significant trials in Ina's life has been balancing her demanding career with her personal life. Her husband, Jeffrey, is a highly respected academic and dean at Yale University, which meant that their relationship often required managing long periods of separation due to his work commitments. Despite these challenges, Ina and Jeffrey's marriage has remained a steadfast source of support and love. Their enduring partnership speaks to their mutual commitment to each other, even when the demands of their respective careers pulled them in different directions.

Ina has also been candid about the moments of self-doubt she faced throughout her journey. At various points in her career, she questioned whether she was capable of achieving the success she desired. In interviews, she has openly acknowledged times when she thought, "I can't do this." Yet, instead of allowing these moments of doubt to define her, Ina chose to persevere. She surrounded herself with a supportive team, trusted her instincts, and continued to push forward, taking calculated risks and embracing new opportunities. Her ability to overcome self-doubt is a testament to her inner strength and unwavering belief in her ability to succeed.

Turning Challenges into Triumphs

Despite the many challenges, Ina's career is a shining example of how resilience and determination can lead to extraordinary success. From her early, uncertain leap into the culinary world to becoming one of the most recognized figures in the food industry, Ina has faced each obstacle with grace and tenacity. Each setback, whether it was the struggle to perfect her cookbook or the pressure of maintaining authenticity in a fast-paced, commercialized world, became an opportunity for growth. Ina's story is one of perseverance, reminding us that success is not defined solely by achievements, but by the ability to rise above difficulties and turn them into triumphs.

This chapter illustrates that Ina Garten's path to success was not a smooth one, but rather a journey shaped by resilience, self-belief, and the ability to turn challenges into learning experiences. Her story is a testament to the power of persistence and the importance of staying true to one's values, no matter the obstacles. Ultimately, Ina has shown that true success is not just about reaching the pinnacle of one's career—it's about overcoming the hurdles along the way and emerging stronger than before.

Chapter 12

The Heart of Ina's Success: A Network of Love and Collaboration

Ina Garten's remarkable career and personal life have been deeply influenced by the people who have stood by her side—those who supported her through every challenge, celebrated her successes, and played pivotal roles in shaping the person she is today. From lifelong friends to professional collaborators, this chapter offers a closer look at the individuals who have contributed to Ina's journey, providing insight into the powerful connections that have enriched both her work and her life.

The Friends Who Became Family

Ina's home in East Hampton has always been more than just a place to cook and entertain; it is a sanctuary for her closest friends and a space where the bonds of friendship are strengthened over shared meals and laughter. Some of Ina's most cherished friendships have become an integral part of her culinary journey.

For instance, her friendship with actor Alec Baldwin is well-known, and he has often appeared in her stories and on her television show. Similarly, designer Patricia Wells, another close friend, frequently joins Ina on-screen and has provided both personal and professional support. These friends are not just a part of Ina's personal life but also serve as a vital part of her creative process. They provide feedback, share in the joy of cooking, and occasionally appear alongside her on *Barefoot Contessa*, adding an authentic touch to the show. Ina's relationships are not merely about socializing—they are a reflection of the warmth, trust, and camaraderie that define her life and work.

Jeffrey: Ina's Unwavering Supporter

If there is one person whose presence has been a constant source of encouragement and inspiration for Ina, it is her husband, Jeffrey Garten. While Ina's career and achievements are a testament to her own talents and drive, Jeffrey's unwavering support has played an indispensable role in her success. Ina often refers to him as her greatest cheerleader, the one person who always believed in her, even during times of self-doubt. His encouragement was instrumental when she made the leap from government service to the culinary world, and it was his steadfast belief in her that motivated her to start *Barefoot Contessa* and embark on a television career. Their shared love of food, travel, and each other has created a strong foundation for both their marriage and Ina's career. Ina often credits Jeffrey as an irreplaceable figure in her life, noting that their partnership has not only enriched her personal life but has also deeply influenced her work.

The Team Behind *Barefoot Contessa*

Behind Ina's polished, approachable cooking style and the visually stunning recipes she shares with the world is a dedicated team of professionals who help bring her creative vision to life. Ina's collaborations with people like photographer Quentin Bacon have been essential to capturing the essence of her work. Bacon's photography has become iconic in Ina's cookbooks, highlighting the beauty and simplicity of the dishes she creates. Editor Maria Guarnaschelli, who helped shape Ina's first cookbook, has also been a key collaborator, refining Ina's recipes and ensuring they were as clear and accessible as possible for readers. These partnerships, built on trust and a shared commitment to quality, have allowed Ina to produce work that is not only informative but visually captivating. In addition to her collaborators, Ina's team of assistants, many of whom have appeared on her television show, plays an essential role in maintaining the high standards of *Barefoot Contessa*. These individuals are more than just employees—they are trusted friends who understand Ina's creative process and contribute to the overall success of her brand. Through these professional relationships, Ina has been able to maintain a balance between her vision and the collaborative efforts that bring it to life.

The East Hampton Community: A Supportive Network

East Hampton is not just the backdrop for Ina's life—it is an integral part of her story. The local community has been a source of inspiration and support throughout her career. From the butchers who provide the finest cuts of meat to the bakers who offer fresh, high-quality ingredients, the vendors of East Hampton have helped shape Ina's culinary philosophy. Her relationships with these local purveyors are a reflection of her belief in supporting small businesses and using the best ingredients available. Ina's commitment to showcasing local producers and championing fresh, seasonal produce is a hallmark of her cooking style, and it reflects her respect for the community that has nurtured her career. These connections extend beyond business transactions—they are built on mutual respect and a shared passion for good food, making the East Hampton community a central part of Ina's journey.

Fans Who Became Friends

One of the most remarkable aspects of Ina's career is her ability to connect with her audience on a personal level. Over the years, Ina has cultivated a loyal fan base that has evolved from mere admirers of her work into genuine friends and collaborators. Through handwritten letters, social media interactions, and even chance encounters, Ina has built lasting relationships with many of her fans. These interactions have been an ongoing source of inspiration for Ina, fueling her creativity and motivating her to continue her work. Her fans have become a vital part of her journey, offering not just praise but also constructive feedback, and reinforcing her mission to make cooking enjoyable and accessible. Ina's ability to make each person feel heard and appreciated has allowed her to create a community of people who share her values and passion for food.

Mentors and Inspirations: Building on the Foundations of Others

While Ina has carved her own path to success, she often credits other culinary icons as being key inspirations in shaping her approach to cooking and entertaining. Figures like Julia Child and Martha Stewart have influenced Ina's focus on technique, presentation, and creating an inviting atmosphere for guests. Ina admires Child's ability to make complex cooking techniques accessible to home cooks and Stewart's knack for elevating everyday tasks with style and grace. These culinary giants helped pave the way for Ina to establish her own brand, but rather than simply following in their footsteps, Ina has taken what she learned from them and adapted it to her own unique style. Her work continues to reflect the principles of quality, elegance, and approachability that these mentors embodied, making their influence evident in everything she does.

A Circle of Love, Support, and Legacy

Ina Garten's inner circle is a testament to the importance of relationships in both personal and professional life. By surrounding herself with people who share her values and passions, she has created a life that reflects the joy and warmth she seeks to bring to others. Her circle—comprising family, friends, colleagues, and fans—is not just a support system but a network that has contributed to her success in countless ways. These individuals have enriched her life, helping to shape the *Barefoot Contessa* brand and ensuring that her work continues to resonate with people from all walks of life. Through these relationships, Ina has built not only a career but a legacy of connection, creativity, and camaraderie. Her inner circle is not just a group of people who helped her get where she is today; it's a community that has shared in her vision and supported her every step of the way, embodying the very spirit of hospitality and generosity that defines Ina Garten.

Chapter 13

Thriving in a Modern Culinary Landscape

The culinary world has undergone dramatic transformations over the years, driven by evolving tastes, advances in technology, and shifts in society's approach to food. Amidst this ever-changing landscape, Ina Garten has remained a constant, adapting to the times without compromising the authenticity and warmth that have become synonymous with her brand. This chapter explores how Ina has navigated these changes, staying relevant in the modern culinary world while preserving the qualities that have made her a beloved figure for home cooks around the globe.

The Power of Social Media: From Hesitation to Embrace

For much of Ina Garten's career, her work was shared through traditional media—cookbooks, television appearances, and personal events. However, the advent of social media fundamentally changed the way audiences interacted with culinary content. Initially hesitant about joining platforms like Instagram,

Ina eventually saw the value in connecting directly with her fans through these channels. Recognizing the opportunity to reach her audience in real-time, she embraced the digital space, using it to showcase her life and cooking in a more intimate way.

Her social media posts, which feature everything from weekend meals to behind-the-scenes moments in her East Hampton kitchen, have struck a chord with millions of followers. Ina's famous catchphrases, like "How easy is that?" and "Store-bought is fine," have taken on new life as memes and hashtags, contributing to her continued relevance in popular culture. Through these interactions, Ina has managed to amplify her reach while remaining true to her genuine, approachable persona. Social media has become a tool for strengthening the sense of connection between Ina and her audience, deepening the bond that has always been central to her success.

Adapting to New Food Trends Without Losing Her Essence

As the food world continues to evolve, new trends and dietary preferences regularly emerge. From plant-based diets to gluten-free cooking, the culinary landscape is constantly shifting, with each trend gaining significant attention in the media. While Ina Garten has never been one to chase after fleeting food trends, she has remained mindful of them and, when appropriate, has incorporated elements of these trends into her recipes.

For instance, Ina has found ways to adapt her classic dishes to accommodate dietary needs, always staying true to her core values of flavor, simplicity, and accessibility. Her focus is on creating recipes that are both satisfying and achievable for home cooks, without succumbing to the pressure to follow every new food fad. Ina's ability to adapt, while maintaining the integrity of her cooking style, has allowed her to remain a relevant and trusted figure in a world where food trends come and go with alarming speed.

Expanding Accessibility: Bringing Good Food to Everyone

Ina has long been an advocate for making good food accessible to all, emphasizing the importance of simple, reliable recipes that anyone can recreate at home. As technology has evolved, so too has the way people access food and cooking resources. With the rise of online grocery shopping, meal delivery services, and virtual cooking classes, Ina has adapted by recommending products and services that align with her philosophy of bringing quality food to everyone, regardless of their circumstances.

Her cookbooks and television shows are now widely available on digital platforms, expanding the reach of her work to a global audience. Ina's adaptability in embracing these new methods of distribution reflects her commitment to making cooking more approachable and accessible to people from all walks of life. Whether it's providing guidance on ingredient substitutions or offering tips for creating delicious meals with pantry staples, Ina's emphasis on accessibility remains a key pillar of her brand.

Cooking Through Crisis: A Comforting Presence in Challenging Times

The global pandemic of 2020 presented a unique set of challenges for the culinary world. As people spent more time at home and cooked their own meals out of necessity, Ina Garten became a source of comfort and inspiration. During this period of uncertainty, Ina's familiar, soothing presence offered a sense of stability. She responded by sharing recipes that utilized pantry staples, helping home cooks navigate a time when access to fresh ingredients was often limited.

Ina's social media presence was also a source of lightheartedness during difficult times. One particularly memorable moment came when she posted a viral video of herself preparing a giant Cosmopolitan cocktail, a playful gesture that resonated with fans and provided a much-needed sense of connection in an otherwise isolating time. Ina's ability to bring joy, levity, and practical advice to her audience during a global crisis was a testament to the comfort and positivity her brand exudes.

Culinary Diversity: Celebrating Global Influences

As food media has evolved, it has become more inclusive, showcasing voices from diverse cultural backgrounds and featuring cuisines from around the world. Ina has embraced this shift by incorporating global influences into her recipes, reflecting her respect for culinary traditions from various cultures. While her training is rooted in French-inspired techniques, Ina has remained open to learning from other food traditions, blending her love for classic dishes with a willingness to experiment and explore new flavors.

This openness to culinary diversity not only enriches her cooking but also demonstrates her belief that food is a universal language—a way to bridge gaps and connect people from different walks of life. Ina's ability to celebrate global influences, while staying true to her own style, has kept her work relevant and exciting in an era where food culture is increasingly diverse and dynamic.

A Lasting Legacy: Inspiring the Next Generation

Ina Garten's influence extends far beyond her current body of work. As the culinary landscape continues to evolve, her ability to adapt while staying true to her core values offers valuable lessons for future chefs, food creators, and influencers. Her enduring popularity suggests that her impact will continue to be felt for generations to come. For aspiring chefs and content creators, Ina's career serves as a model of how to build a meaningful, authentic brand that resonates with people across different platforms and generations.

Ina's adaptability, generosity, and unwavering commitment to quality have made her not just a culinary icon but a role model for navigating a rapidly changing world. She has shown that it's possible to thrive in the face of uncertainty by staying true to one's passions and values while embracing the opportunities that change brings.

Looking Ahead: The Future of *Barefoot Contessa*

As Ina Garten reflects on the future, her focus remains clear: to continue sharing the joy of cooking, creating recipes that inspire, and fostering a sense of connection through good food and good company. Whether through her cookbooks, new media ventures, or other creative pursuits, Ina is poised to continue making an impact in the culinary world for years to come. Her brand will undoubtedly continue to evolve, but the core values that have made her so beloved—authenticity, simplicity, and a genuine love of food—will remain unchanged.

Ina Garten's ability to adapt to a changing world while staying true to herself is a testament to her enduring success. Through her adaptability, passion, and commitment to quality, she has not only kept up with a shifting culinary landscape but has shown the world how to thrive within it.

Epilogue

A Legacy of Connection Through Food

As the warm, savory aroma of roasted chicken fills the air and a beautifully arranged table gleams softly under the glow of flickering candles, the essence of Ina Garten's philosophy comes to life. Her influence stretches far beyond the dishes she's prepared or the pages of her cookbooks. What she has truly built is a bridge—connecting people, their kitchens, and the simple joy of sharing a meal.

Ina Garten's incredible journey, from her early days in Washington, D.C., working behind a desk to becoming a culinary icon adored by millions, is a testament to her authenticity and passion. She never sought fame or chased fleeting trends; instead, she created a career founded on the belief that cooking should be about bringing happiness to both those who create and those who share in the experience. Ina's trademark style of unpretentious elegance, combined with her genuine warmth, has made her a trusted companion in kitchens across the world, making her both a culinary guide and a friend to many.

As the world of food continues to change, Ina's influence remains steadfast and timeless. Her recipes, which celebrate simplicity, flavor, and the joy of sharing a meal, continue to inspire home cooks to embrace the art of cooking, often encouraging them to gather around the table with loved ones. Her well-known catchphrase, "How easy is that?" has become more than just words; it's a reminder to approach cooking—and life—with ease and joy, taking on challenges with a light heart, whether in the kitchen or in other areas of life.

Looking toward the future, Ina's legacy is firmly rooted not only in the cookbooks that continue to adorn shelves and the television reruns that provide comfort to viewers, but also in the lasting memories she has helped create. From quiet, intimate dinners to lively celebrations, Ina's recipes and her approach to life will continue to find their place at tables for generations. She has given us more than just food; she's given us the tools to create experiences, to gather together, and to savor the simple pleasures of life.

The "Legacy of Connection Through Food" is not just Ina's—it's ours. It's a table filled with love, laughter, and the ongoing reminder that food is one of the greatest joys of life. As Ina herself would surely say, "Isn't that what it's all about?" And so, the table she's set for us remains, inviting us to pull up a chair and savor life's simple pleasures, one delicious meal at a time.

Made in United States
Orlando, FL
16 March 2025